# Fractured Voices:

# Breaking the Silence

### Helen Wheeler, Ed

To Michelle, my guiding light at the dark edge of my soul. Thank you.

FRACTURED VOICES: BREAKING THE SILENCE
 Helen Wheeler and Victoria Villasenor, Ed.
 Nicci Robinson, Copy Editor
 Global Words Press
 Copyright retained by individual authors
 Cover Photo by Roy McPartland
 Cover Design by Pippa Hennessy
 Internal Artwork Copyright retained by Artists
 Collection copyright © 2015 Global Words Press
 Imprint Digital, UK
 Cataloging information
 ISBN: 978-0-9929354-8-1

# FRACTURED VOICES: BREAKING THE SILENCE

## HELEN WHEELER, ED

2015
GLOBAL WORDS PRESS
NOTTINGHAM, UK

# FOREWORD

ISAS was established in 1991 by Newark and Sherwood Volunteer Services, Health, Women's Aid and other organisations who began to realise the rising need for the provision of specialist counselling for female survivors. It was soon recognised that there were male survivors also in need of such provision. ISAS remains the only service in Nottinghamshire that delivers to both male and female survivors.

Throughout the 25 years we have been providing services, we have worked with clients in many settings, including prisons and more recently, in schools and community settings. We provide one-to-one therapy, group therapy, drumming and drama therapy, to name but a few of the innovative ways we support survivors.

The Creative Writing Group 'Fractured Voices' was the brain child of one of our counsellors, Helen Wheeler. Whilst looking for other vehicles for our clients to express their thoughts and feelings, the group was established with a small pot of funding from the People's Health Trust and Nottingham Equal.

The group has grown from strength to strength, and clients meet in a relaxed and creative atmosphere, enabling them to express themselves freely and without fear.

The publication of this book is a testimony to our clients; the damaged and brave souls that entrust us with their deepest, darkest secrets. What an honour and privilege to know we travel with them on their healing journey every day.

~Jo Butler,
Director

# PREFACE

Fractured Voices began as an idea to bring survivors together on a therapeutic journey to find their voices. This book is a collaboration of written work, spoken words and art arising from a series of Holistic Creative Discourse sessions and workshops run by myself at ISAS, Nottingham.

It is about telling stories which are raw and from the heart. It's about finally mending voices and learning how to speak, sing or, sometimes, even scream. Every word here has been written by someone who has survived childhood sexual abuse or incest. Many survivors have suffered judgement and prejudice along the way, and all were silenced.

Fractured Voices is about beginning to redress the balance, evening up the playing field, and giving hope. Hope to those who contribute, and hope to those who read it. Hope that your story can be told, that you will be heard, and you do exist! It's about breaking the silence and telling your story.

~Helen Wheeler MA,
UKCP Accred Psychotherapist
Creative Writing Group Lead

18/Eyesight: Glimpsing Reality/ The Depths Of Trauma -
A Fractured Mind, Body, and Soul
by Anonymous

# CONTENTS

# CHAPTER ONE: POEMS

Don't hurt us.

By Angela McKenzie

**BELIEVING**
by Usha

Deeply scared...
Forever afraid...
Dazed by selfish acts of unkindness...
Darkness and dampness and a detrimental chill...
This is no life to be leading....
I summon my demons to heavens gates
Re-script my past journey...
From here on out
I am in control
Believing...

## BUTTERFLY
by Usha

What has this all been about?
The fear, the shame, the guilt ridden hype?
Why does everything feel so wrong?
My soul tells me I have the right
To be happy, and free of this earthly debt.

Why do I have to carry
This mountain everywhere I go?
My back hurts now and my thighs are toned enough,
So time to put that mountain down.
So I can climb up it!

Where do I start?
Well, invest in a solid pair of footwear,
Be warm and hydrated,
Be safe and stay grounded,
I wish you all the luck.

Ok, I'm off!
World here I come!
I'm no longer living in a cocoon,
I've transformed,
Now flying high.

I have a choice and a freedom
I have fought long and hard
A beautiful victory.

## EQUILIBRIUM
by Usha

High pitch!
Low pitch!
Daggers!
Or bullets!
A shark or
A crocodile
Light or dark
All I want is peace of mind
And balance
From that I can find
My peace and move on
Forward with my life
Equilibrium....

## FROM DARKNESS TO THE LIGHT
by Usha

Silenced by shame, guilt, afraid to voice my feelings.
Isolated by others, through trauma of others.
Kept in the dark till the time has felt right.
Hovering between worlds of disillusion and fear, hoping I can turn this awful experience into a positive one.
Gazing out my window, wondering if I'll ever be free from this burden I've carried for too long.
Incredibly determined to release this pain naturally and without causing others harm along the way.
Realising that my life's passion/dreams can come true, but I have much work to do on my self awareness and self-love in order to proceed with panache.
Loving myself to my very roots has allowed me to forgive and move forward from this past pain I'd carried for decades.

## FROM FEAR TO FAITH
by Usha

- I was thrown off the top of a cliff (unaided)
- I was eaten by a shark and left for dead
- I was pecked at for 4 years every day by hungry vultures
- I was trampled over by a herd of rhino's, elephants and horses
- I was jammed between a vice for 18 years
- I was the black sheep amongst the white sheep
- I was scalded by a hot iron to my head
- My hands, feet, and mouth were stolen from me and sold without my consent
- I was chucked into an ocean and I had no idea how to swim or which direction to go in

I imagine floats and a super jet on my back to trust I would not sink. So I moved slowly and as I did, I got faster and faster, stronger and stronger, lighter and lighter. Being in the ocean cleansed my soul. My wounds were being washed away and healed! Thank you spirit, for your faith in me.

I made it onto solid ground, my feet touched soft sand, and the sun's warm glow penetrated my being. A deep breath and an overwhelming feeling of joy. I learnt how to swim. With the power I was born with I reclaimed and manifested a new beginning, a beautiful life full of abundance. It's my birth right to be happy, the universe told me so, and I believe it.

Sweet universe, thank you for blessing me with laughter and the opportunity to live and experience a life I wish to manifest. I am now flying high through love, light and determination to just be.

Thank you.

## KARMA
### by Usha

I know I'm only an Indian child
I didn't want to do this
I know it's wrong.
Why can't anybody else see that?
May be they are all right
And I am wrong.
Yes, it's probably the case,
As I am only a child,
An Indian girl with no value.
Please god help me stay strong
I'm an adult now,
I was right all along!
It was wrong.
And they were all wrong
Clearly dysfunctional people
To think that this act of abuse
Was normal...
And rumour has it
That all these dysfunctional people
Are living a hellish life
Due to the burdens they put on me.
Karma...

## MY HIGHER SELF
by Usha

Where does this pain end?
What's feeding it to stay alive in me?
What am I going to do to put an end to it?
Will I allow this demon to follow me into my future?

Can I really make the choice?
Will I make a stand?
Yes, I will!

Today I begin my journey to change my life around,
Simply because I am worth it!
It's my birth right to be happy,
And to love and be loved.

## MOVING FORWARD
by Usha

As I slowly watch the world go by
I witness all my past wounds heal,
as though they were never created.
And the pain, deceit, selfishness,
Dishonesty, physical abuse, never occurred.
As I stand here in my present state of mind,
I discover self-love,

The most powerful tool in existence,
And with this blessing of self-love a
Wonderful new creation was formed.
I cannot change my past
But through my mind's eye
I created difference.
In each and every encounter displayed to me
I forgive my past,
Embrace my future,
And enjoy my here and now
with unlimited abundance,
love, light, and much peace.
I turned my fears into ants,
And my joys into appreciation.
And it all emerged into
I am who I am.
Helping those see light
Through their distorted visions,

Enables me to grow
Into the being I wish to be.

Through all my trials and tribulations
I am free.

As I've worked hard
Day and night,
To cultivate my foundations,
I magically have the power
To eliminate that which serves no purpose.
With gratitude for the opportunity indeed,
Forever will I learn?
Thank you universe, spirit god,
And my beautiful angels for
Your unconditional love, support, and wisdom.
You shine on me
Every, single, blessed day.

## THE RIGHT WAY
by Usha

Where does the abuse actually end?
Who will be the one to make that positive difference?
How has any woman or child suffered sexual abuse
By these human beings?
My heart aches, as though Hercules is
Squeezing it with both hands.
They sexually abused me time and time again,
My eyes feel permanently drowned.
Was he abused? Is that why he decided to hurt me?
You shouldn't do this, I'm like a daughter to you!
Why can't you hear me?
God, please help these men
With their demons to stop abusing.
Let them see that what they are doing
Is an act of injustice.
They will have to pay
For the sins they have committed.
Please help them open their eyes,
Before they go back to heaven.

## WARRIOR NATION
by Usha

Saddened by the fact that I am trapped and I can't talk about how badly I've been treated; it's hard to justify. I've been the one to blame, because I am a Sikh girl and girls are treated very different to Sikh boys.

Imprisoned by speaking my truth because of the drilled-in fear of being abandoned by people that don't even care. Just to keep face in society.

Kissed by my angels, to shift myself forward, to speak of my emotions, the physical and sexual abuse, with the intention of peace and transformation.

Having courage and faith to make a difference to me, and maybe others, too.

Giving myself permission to assert myself well, and release this shame and the detrimental feelings of suicide.

Insecure, blaming myself, asking myself if what happened was no biggy! Justifying it all because 'it's normal to do that, it's ok.'

Exchanging my freewill for silence. Those bastards were wrong, not me.

Relentless behaviour, their sick thoughts, more than one, becomes a question to my judgement of myself. Weakened by these self-destructive thoughts, it kept me feeling suicidal beyond belief...I'm dirty, I'm a slag, I'm a drama queen, I'm insecure, I'm the one who didn't stop it, so it's my fault.

No, it's not...

Lovingly asserting myself, because these abusers do not deserve any of my time. They're getting on with their lives and I'm supposed to stay in the well of Hell! I really do not think so. I no longer allow myself to be hurt, manipulated, guilt ridden, shamed disrespected, humiliated, or hurt in any way. Why? Because I am a free spirit who deserves to live with love, light, happiness, and freedom of speech. I owe it to me.

## CHILDCARE
by Karen

Cocoon myself in my bed like a frightened child who needs their
rest...
Hoping that I'll sleep tonight instead of being woken while it's
dark ...
I've never really felt safe at night, cause sometimes nights never
really feel right...
Light, I need to keep me safe while I sleep so silently...
Depression, I'm in a mental state of gloom feeling low and in an
unhappy place...
Choke, is the feeling of being strangled or smothered while I
sleep...
Anxious, worried and tense, it's how you made me feel ...
Remorse, he shown no remorse, he had no feeling of sorrow or
Regret for the pain he was causing...
Escape, hoping to feel free for relaxation, I hope to find some day.

## DOVES FLY
by Karen

Deaf, I thought my abuse would fall on deaf ears
No one would want to listen
Or take notice of what he was doing...
Obeying the control he had over me
Carrying out the instructions
And orders he gives to me...
Voice, which I heard in my head.
Please be brave, go and tell someone...
Echoes through the night
You can hear them cry...
Safe, put them out of harm's way
And out of danger...
Flock, like seagulls I can fly so high
Free at last. I shout so loud
While I'm high in the sky...
Light, is what I see
At the end of the tunnel and
Hope and happiness
Are waiting for me ...
Years of pain, years of sorrow.
I can reach out now and say
There's a bright tomorrow.

### HOW HE MADE ME FEEL
by Karen

He made me feel cheap,
He made me feel dirty.
For what he wanted me to do,
And how he wanted me to do it.
It didn't matter where,
It didn't matter when.
As long as he got what he wanted,
He couldn't care less.
As long as he didn't get caught.
He disgusts me, he makes me feel sick.
I'm so ashamed for ever calling you Dad.

## My Anger
### by Karen

I look like I am happy, but really I'm not.
Because all of my anger just won't stop.
I tell people I'm fine, but I know I'm not.
I'm going for help, to make it stop.
Sometimes I'll make out it's working,
But really, it's not.
I still see him looking at me while he's hurting me lots.
I feel he's inside me, this scares me a lot.
I just want this feeling to go. Will it ever stop?
My anger makes me feel like trashing the house.
My anger makes me feel all scared inside.
My anger makes me want to scream and shout.
My anger makes me feel as if I just want to cry.

## THE PLACE I GREW UP
by Karen

My place was busy with family doing everyday stuff
My place has food, but most times has none
We mainly go hungry and so did mum
'Cause he'd take the money and go to the pub
Leaving us cold and without a fire
Then he'd come home, making the house smell of stale beer and cider
It made us scared and very anxious.

### TOP GUN
by Karen

Tiny steps it will take to make things a lot better...
Overcome, you're starting to take control of your life...
Picking up the pieces and putting them in the right order...
Gaining back your courage, your confidence, and your ability to speak out...
Understanding what is right, and what is wrong...
Nightmares, knowing that one day you'll have sweet dreams instead
      Your nightmares will soon be over.....

## WARRIORS
by Karen

Wicked, evil, and sinful things you did and
The harm you wanted to cause...
Afraid, because I'm frightened of
Being alone in the dark...

Rash, careless, without thinking
What might happen to me...
Reprove to tell somebody
He's done wrong...

Idiot, I was a stupid child for keeping
It to myself...
Outrage, of the cruel and violent things
He's done...

Reveal the secrets that I'd kept
For so long...
Scars are marked in my mind and
My heart will never heal...

They will always be there
They will never go away...

## A LIVING SURVIVOR
by Anonymous

When I was a child I was the genuine victim
Of a horrific crime,
I didn't plan it, cause it, commit it, or deserve it,
and with a fight, without remorse, he served his time.

And I've been strong enough to overcome the collateral damage.
That's why,
I am a living survivor.

Can you empathize?
Do you feel you're good enough inside?
Can you lose control and step out of the shadows,
Which hide your eyes?

Underneath our skin, we're all flesh and bones,
'neath those scars, there's a heart longing for home.
Are you entitled?
Am I expected to comply to your every command?
And can you connect with somebody who just don't understand?

Who needs a hand after they learnt to hold their own?
Let it be known,
 'neath these scars, a heart longed for home.

### DEEP DARK BLACK HOLE
by Anonymous

I used to live down the bottom of a deep and dark,
Black and deathly, hole.
Throw a ladder down now,
I'm up on the ground, in the sunshine,
And all the smiling people crowding around,
And we, no, we don't look down.

Looking back at those empty years,
I was stuck in my fears,
Down, down, in the dark,
Seemed safer to hide,
When my mind wasn't ever really my own.
But I've come out now into the light,
Through those storms we go through in life.

You can't fly higher than you can conceive
In your own dreams.
She said to me, the wisest one
Has always been burnt the worst, it seems,
But don't get stuck in pity,
and don't you ever give up on me.

### INSIDE
by Angela

Here is my pain
Staring me straight in the face
Here is my pain
Inside, am I
Can you see me?
Hear me scream
'Save me, save me'
Here is my pain
Who are you, girl?
Pretending woman
Who are you, little girl?
BIg smile
Loud laugh
Silent screams

## GRIEF
by Angela

I felt its presence behind my ribs
And everything ground to a halt

Huge hands snapped and split my sternum
Ripped and gripped my heart
Squeezing bloody tears from my eyes

Heard you whispering in the shadows
"Don't forget me, don't forget me."
Felt you standing silently behind me

Felt the grip constrict my neck
And I couldn't turn to look
Couldn't see to find
My happiness

Funny babbles in my ear
Fill me with fear
Lies and filth poured out
From your poisoned mouth
Stupid, shallow smile at me
To mask your hidden treachery
Behind your eyes I see no soul

Foolish I
Who gave you my red gold?
The night your eye killed me
Came crashing through my skeleton
With its Cyclops fury.

## EVERY PART OF ME
by Anonymous

Friend or foe, it was so hard to know,
It's taken years to see,
How you managed to fool
Every part of me.
How you crept around and
Wound your way in,
Privately planning
And calculating under the dim.
Contaminating this body
Down to its bones,
Chaining me in shackles,
So no one would know.

To steal my soul with your
cherry ChapStick charms,
To blind my vision,
And keep me unarmed.

You tried to take my shine
By possessing my mind,
But you get what you give,
All you got is empty alibis.
How you silenced my soul
With your glaring cold eyes,
While disguising your demons,
With pretty white lies.

Tightening your hands
That were clasped around my neck,
No-never breathe the truth,
Was the clear message you sent.
To steal my heart
With your cherry ChapStick charms,
By poisoning my blood,
And tying my hands.
You tried to take my shine
By stealing my mind,
But you get what you give,
All you got is empty alibis.

### ISAS
by Karen

**I** is for innocence: the innocence I have lost,
battered and bruised, and sexually abused.
By someone I should have trusted.

**S** is for secrets: secrets not to be told,
I kept them deep, thinking,
it's all my fault.

**A** is for anger: the anger inside,
the pain and sorrow
that he's left behind.

**S** is for speak: or shout it out loud
    HEY, YOU NASTY MAN
    THIS IS NOT ALLOWED

'Cause now I'm with ISAS they've shown me the way,
to make things better,
and lift that dark cloud.

## BRAVE NEW WORLD
by Karen

Brave is the girl that I have become,
For being so brave
                and telling my mum, what he had done.
I need to feel like new inside
Instead of like taking a very bad pill
Like what I've had for so many years
                But now I'm shedding no more tears,
Hoping to chase away all that fear
Our world was so far but now so near
I've found someone so very dear.
He keeps me so close and away from fear
                And he'll stay in my heart forever and ever.

### STUCK INSIDE/FREE LOVE/A THOUSAND CHANGING FACES
by Anonymous

Stuck inside when I gave my love to you freely,
Opened up and I trusted you completely,
Put me down, hold my head in your shame,
'cause I fell into playing your twisted games.
Now it's me, who projects the pain,
'cause inside I took on the blame.

Self-destruct or hide away,
I'm no good anyway,
Help me, I wish I could say.

What can I do to make you love me?
Wear a hundred changing faces discreetly?
But baby, I can't make you believe me,
Oh no, I can't make you believe me.

You're a cheat, but I didn't follow the rules,
Oh man, oh man, how I'm feeling the fool,
I thought I knew you.
You're deluded, but I didn't say no to taboo,
Oh man, oh man, how I depended on you.

You're a liar, but I didn't speak my own truth,
Oh man, oh man, oh man,
How I thought I could trust you.

What can I do to make you love me?
And if you do, will it even fulfil me?

Or am I wanting to express who I am really,
Oh yes, oh yes, who I am really.

Stuck inside when I saw you a little more clearly,
My eyes un-blind, my heart broken completely,
Stab my back and I fell to the floor,
I told the truth, I wasn't protecting you no more.

Now it's me, who's locking the doors,
'Cause inside I was smashed to the core.
An ivory tower, throw away the key,
Please don't touch me,
I just want to feel safety,
In a warm, dark place, let me be.

# CHAPTER TWO: LETTERS

By Angela McKenzie

## MY LETTER OF GRATITUDE
### by Usha

I will never forget the very first day I went to ISAS for an interview. My times had been mixed up, but this was no coincidence at all. It was divinely organised to meet my counsellor, and these wonderful human beings who have provided such a phenomenal service to the world. I was petrified to open up this can of worms, but had a warm feeling that these people were going to help me break through all these suppressed feelings. Nine months later I feel as light as a feather, how is this possible? For years I've carried the burden around with me out of guilt, shame and respect. But it did me no justice. I wanted to live, not just survive, and so I took a huge leap of faith and never looked back. As daunting and detrimental as it became, I kept on moving with the support of my amazing spiritual counsellor, who helped me move mountains. For nine months my counsellor has been my rock and my much needed earth angel. I love you, ISAS, for bringing my spirit back to life. Your organisation is a wonderful asset to Nottingham, without a single doubt. Without your magical guidance, warm love, and genuine desire to help others, who knows where any of us would be now? ISAS is a divine saviour in an earthly form. Thank you so much, I will be forever grateful to you for all your help. You are all so amazing and blessed to have the gift you all have in helping others. From all of us learning to grow at ISAS, a massive thank you, big love, light, and so much peace.

## WHAT REMAINS?
by Andrew

To Dum and Mad,

It feels strange writing to you in this way, as if we are strangers. Maybe you will find what I have to tell you strange, or unbelievable, but I have decided to tell you anyway, or at least, even if you never see this, to put this on record, as a kind of monument, in case it is needed. It feels like an aggressive act to withhold it from you when I feel that in some way you have a right to know why I do not see you much, why we are not close. At least, from my side. But it is also a violent act to tell you, so it is your choice whether you read on or not. If you do, I warn you now, you are not going to like it.

I think of the pattern of my life differently to how I imagine you see it. It does not have the typical 'beginning, middle and end' format. For me, it is as if my life only really started a few years ago, as if up until that point it was only a half-life, vaguely unconnected with my essential self. I had always felt like that, as far back as I could remember. I can recall how this dramatic change came about very clearly. It was night time and I was in bed, asleep, but I was dreaming. In my dream I was back at school. It was not me as I really am, or really was as a child, but a pig-like creature, fat and coarse and bristly, but with a human head, the head of a child, sweet and innocent and smiling. There was a group of smartly dressed young women around me, silhouetted against the high windows of the classroom, dressed in the style of the early 1960s, when I was at school, with patterned dresses and beehive hairdos. I assume they were teachers. I was amusing them with my innocent piggy antics, and they were laughing at me, a bit patronising. They were cool and smoking cigarettes and more interested in the dry wit of their chatter than in me. I scurried about for a bit on the parquet floor of the classroom, and then, realising the teachers had lost interest in me, slipped away, down the stairs and out of the building, across the dry, wide playground and into the toilet. I wasn't a pig anymore, I was me as I really was, and the toilet was not strange like in a dream, as everything had been before, but very real, with the feel and smells of the toilet, my smells...and his smells. The smell of his tobacco, and the look he gave me over the toilet door, the look of control, that told me he could do what he wanted and I could not stop him. It wasn't a dream anymore but a memory, and I was awake now, remembering, disoriented, staring hard into the darkness, living it again. Something had really happened, more real than any other memory I had ever had, making more sense than any other memory I had ever had.

I was hot and sweating and shaking. I got up and went downstairs, left my wife sleeping in bed. I was half-upset and half-thinking with a ferocious clarity, able to see straightaway that this was the key to unlock the mystery of my fucked-up life, literally fucked-up, by that teacher, a man I should have been able to trust. Ludicrously he was the school's 'dirty old man', the teacher who encouraged the girls to do handstands so he could look at their knickers, and hit the boys far too hard. I still haven't remembered what he said to me, or even if he said anything at all. But I remember what I said to myself as I walked slowly back across the wide expanse of the playground, back to my classroom, about how I had to pack what had happened away inside me, and never tell anyone, ever.

I got ready for work in silence and left the house. When I got there I realised I was about two hours early. It was still dark. I let myself in and sat and waited for my colleagues to turn up, telling myself things would be okay, that somehow I could carry on, keeping it all contained inside. But when they did turn up, I found I couldn't talk to them without bursting into tears, and realised that my silly veneer of normality was masking deep shock, and I had to go back home to try to sort myself out.

56

From the time of that flashback of what happened to me as a child, to the present, has been almost exactly eight years. For the last year or so, things have calmed down in my quest to try to understand myself anew in the light of the revelation of that night. Over those eight years other memories have surfaced, sometimes again in violent flashbacks, sometimes more insidiously, a slow unfolding of embodied information. These created a full picture of events, not only at the time of the rape itself, but of the chaos that my life became afterwards.

The memory filled in so many gaps in the jigsaw of my understanding of myself. It even made sense that I had to wait so long, until I was fifty years old, to remember something that happened to me when I was eight. I just wasn't ready before, I didn't have what I needed around me. It explained the years of self-loathing, and depression, of course. It explained the extreme physical shyness. It explained why my relationships always seemed to be with other abuse survivors, even though I wasn't conscious of myself as such, as if we could smell it on each other. It explained the drinking, the risk-taking, the promiscuity, the extreme sense of being spoiled in some unspeakable and immutable way, as if there was a stain across me. My deepest fear was that this was knowable by others, though it was hidden to me, that all my attempts to hide my spoiled identity were worthless.

There were very precise things, too. I remember telling a doctor how I couldn't get a song out of my head, the Moody Blues singing 'Go Now'. It was so insistent it felt like a command, telling me to literally leave my new family, to go out into a wilderness until I became indiscernible from the dust, and blew away in the wind. When eventually I checked, I found the song was number one in the pop charts at the time I was raped. Maybe it was playing somewhere in the background?

I am reassured. When I have tried to write to you like this before, my words have been so full of anger and hate that I have known that our relationship, such as it is, could never survive exposing you to them. This feels more measured. This comforts me, it feels like progress. There is no point telling you unless I make you aware of at least some of the horror I have experienced.

I have done so much work, all unseen by you, to try to get myself through this process, what I call my recovery, to get to where I am today. Like ripples expanding on the surface of the lake, the focus shifts away from the incident itself to the context in which it occurred. I do not deny that I have had support from those around me, which has been immensely valuable. In this, and in so many other ways, I have a very great deal to be grateful for, and I *am* grateful. But at heart I have known that this would be a lonely road, but then it always has, since I was raped as an eight-year old child. There is obviously a lot more I could say, a lot more detail I could give, but that is not what concerns me now, that is not what I am left with. For a long time I had to keep asking myself why I had been chosen, what made me such a perfect victim for him? I know it would not be difficult for a cynical adult to identify a vulnerable child, the kind of child who would do as they are told and keep their mouth shut. But what made me that kind of child? And afterwards, in spite of my silence, why did no-one see and wonder at the cause of the distress that I was expressing in so many other ways?

One never imagines that the preoccupations of adulthood will be so rooted in childhood. I am an old man with grown-up children of my own. In a few weeks I retire after 36 years working as a nurse, not a positive career choice in hindsight, but the wounded part of me made it inevitable.

So I still wonder why you did not look after me as you should have. The pain that comes from the sense that I was not loved, or was unlovable, still burns. And finally, I have to ask, if somehow, by some miracle, we could turn the clock back and all live it again, but knowing what we know now, and knowing you as I do, as an adult, would you do anything differently?

## LETTER TO KAREN
by Karen

Dear Karen,

What I am doing is to ease my mind; I am seeing a therapist just so I can talk to someone. Her name is Sue, and I see her once a week. I've finally started to open up, to tell her what I have been through. I can't talk to my family, as I don't know if they would understand. I am married now, with three children, and I think my family would probably think I've moved on. Well, really, in a way I have, but in my mind he will always be there, and there is nothing I can do about that. But what I am doing is helping me a lot. I am also seeing Helen, she's my group therapist, and she helps me share with the group and write my feelings down. We are trying to put a book together to let people have some idea of what our lives have been like. To let them know if they have been through the same thing, there is no need to be scared, they should tell someone like a close friend, neighbour, or better still, a doctor, as you can do that in confidence. One to one, he or she will not tell unless you want them to. I told my doctor I had been suffering for years, and she put me on the right track. Now, with her help, I am starting to see the light at the end of the tunnel. I am hoping for a fresh start, like starting my life all over again, but this one is going to be better.

# Chapter Three:
# Journals and Diaries

By Angela McKenzie

## MY FIRST TASTE (1967-1968)
by Karen

I was about three or four when I had my first taste of sex. That was when Dad took my sister and I for a walk. I thought we were going to watch people bowling on the bowling green. But instead we went into the woods.
This is how it happened...

My sister went off to play in the woods. I was going to join her but Dad asked me to stay with him to help him find wood. So I said "ok" and by this time my sister was off playing. Then he turned and asked me if, before we looked for wood, I'd like a lollipop, as he only had one. I said, "yes please," and he told me I would have to find it, as it was in his trouser pocket. When I put my hand in his pocket I took it out and told him I couldn't find anything, so he asked me to try the other pocket. So I placed my hand in the other. This one had a big hole in it, and when I reached in all I could feel was his penis. I quickly removed my hand and told him I couldn't find anything.

He told me to try again; I looked at him and said, "No, I want to go home."

Dad took hold of my hand and put it back in his pocket, then he started to make me rub, and when he started to feel himself being satisfied, he then told me to take his penis out and place it in my mouth. He started thrusting himself back and forth slowly.

Then I started to feel sick and wanted him to stop, but instead he just got faster and thrust himself a little harder until he was done. He took himself away from me, got himself together, then told me to find my sister, as we were going home.

But before I went to look for her he told me not to say a word or he would kill me. I was so scared I was crying. I found my sister and told her we were going home but she wanted to play. I said, "No, come on, we're going home."

## The Days She Was Away (1968)

It was the year 1968, November time, and Mum took poorly. Or so I thought. I didn't know she was in labour with my little brother, but she was, so the lady next door took my brothers to school as normal. Me and my sister stayed at home with Dad. Mum had to go to hospital on her own; he said he had to look after us.

But anyway, Mum was having her baby, my brothers were at school, and we were at home with him. Everything was alright until half way through the day, when my sister and I were on the floor in front of Dad, where he could see us playing. Then he turned and asked me if I would like to play horses on his knee while my sister was playing on the floor. I said, "yes" getting all excited and happy because I was going to play horses on my dad's knee, and my sister wasn't. I jumped up onto his knee, then started to playfully jump. Dad told me to settle down for a while as he'd got to sort himself out. As I waited I could feel him messing around with the zipper on his pants, then he told me to lift myself on top of his knee as he had to put himself into place. While he was doing this I was trying to look to see what he was doing. When I saw his manhood I wanted to get down, but he told me I was all right and he wasn't going to hurt me, to sit down on him. I gently eased myself down but jumped back up again when I felt his skin touch mine. I looked at my dad and started crying and telling him I wanted my mum to come home. He then just looked at me while putting himself away.

He put me on the floor with my sister, then started calling me a mardy little cry baby, always crying for her mummy. Then as he got up out of his seat to go, he bent down to me and told me to stop crying or he'd give me something to cry for. And if I told anyone, like Mum or my friends, he'd kill me. This made me scared as my sister and I were alone with him. I used to go to bed at night praying for Mum to come home.

## My First Days at School (1969)

I was about 5 years old, and it was my first day of school. I was really excited, I couldn't wait to get to school, but I was also a little scared as well. My brothers told me the teachers were nice, but when I got to school and it was time for Mum to leave, I started to cry. I didn't want her to leave me as I didn't think I would see her again and I'd be there forever. The teacher calmed me down and told me that Mum would pick me up later when school had finished, so Mum went home.

When she got home, Mum told Dad that I was a little upset, then told him it maybe because it was my first day and I was a little nervous. I think she was hoping Dad would turn around and say that everything would be all right. But no, it caused an argument instead. When I came home from school the first thing that came out of his mouth was, "Do you need your dummy?" I looked at Mum, then Dad said, "Yes, I'm talking to you, you mardy cry baby! Won't let go of mummy's apron strings."

I just sat on the settee with my brothers and sister, watching TV with my eyes welling up with tears.

The following day at school I was a little more settled, but when Mum left me, I waved to her, then went into the Wendy house for a cry. A new girl came up to me and relaxed me by asking me to play, and was chasing me around the playground. I felt safe when we got home, because I was with mum and my brothers, but also scared and hurt inside; it felt like I was crying without people seeing...

## My Days as a Junior

Six years old now. I'm a Junior, and I get excited by new friends, but this time I'm not taking them home. My new teacher was a man, Mr Thomas. He was a nice teacher, kind, and always had a smile for the class. One day in class I felt a little uneasy, as I needed to go to ask the teacher a question on the subject I was set to do. Instead, I'd sat at my desk and tried to work it out myself, but Mr Thomas could see I was a little puzzled and confused with my work, so he came and sat on the chair next to me. And oh my God, I was scared. I had pains in my belly and my eyes started welling up. He touched my hand and told me not to be frightened, that he wasn't the Big Bad Wolf! Then he asked me if I needed help with my work, as I was looking a little confused. I said, "yes" and he helped me, then left me alone to get on with the rest on my own.

**No Fireworks Night (1979)**
Bonfire night. We'd never had fireworks, but we'd sit in the back yard and watch next door's, and everyone else, who had fireworks. But we had a laugh and we were happy. Next door offered us a sparkler and an apple but we had to wait until Dad said it was ok. I was at the age where I wasn't bothered about fireworks, I just wanted to go out and away from the house so Sharron and I would go for walks. I tried staying out of Dad's way as much as I could, as I was getting a little older. This didn't bother him because he knew every chance he got, he he could have me, because we were always going to be in the same place, one way or another.

**My Poorly Mamma (1979)**
It was about one and a half weeks after bonfire night, and Mum got word of my mamma being taken ill and was in hospital. This meant Mum was going to see her as my mamma had asked for her. This was ok, because I knew if I couldn't go with Mum, I'd have Sharron to go out with. But Sharron was going somewhere with her sister. I asked Mum if I could go to see mamma with her, but she told me she had already asked Raymond to go. I said, "Okay, I'll just go out and wait for Sharron to come back." But Dad said he needed someone to look after Susan and Sean (my younger brother and sister), while he went out . I told them that Susan was at her mate's, then Dad turned around and said Sean still needed looking after. I asked if I could be shouted down when Dad went out.

He said no, so I was left at home alone with Dad and my little brother. When Mum had gone, Dad asked if I would make a drink. I went into the kitchen put the kettle on. I felt okay because Sean was in the next room. But Dad followed me into the kitchen. I didn't think anything of it, because I knew Sharron would be there soon, but I was wrong. Dad grabbed me from behind. I swung round, told him to leave me alone or I'd shout for Sean.

He told me to go ahead and shout while he kept touching me. I was begging him to stop, but he wouldn't, so I shouted for Sean to help me. He came into the kitchen and asked what I wanted. Dad just turned around and said I didn't mean to shout, and that he should carry on playing. When Sean went back into the living room my Dad wrestled me down onto the floor, then put his hands around my throat and squeezed my neck tight. I almost passed out, my body went hot and sweaty and I started breathing funny and panicky. To make him stop I pretended to pass out, and I thought that would stop him touching me, but I was wrong. He started to lift up my shirt and started pulling down my pants, and the sound of satisfaction in his voice made me feel sick.
I decided to 'wake up,' and I hit him around the face and got to my feet. By this time he'd taken hold of me, slammed me up against the kitchen sink, put his hand over my mouth so I didn't cry out, then said, "I told you not to say anything."
I was absolutely scared, then he started to have sex with me. When he'd finished, he gave me a towel to wipe myself, then told me to keep my mouth shut. Then he went to the pub.

## What's Going Through My Head Every Day
I was about three, maybe four years old, when I witnessed the violent rape and sexual act my dad did to my mum. It was horrible; he'd half undressed her, as he was himself. He couldn't actually reach what part of the body he wanted, as he's a little shorter than my mum. So he'd dragged her from where he was attacking her to his chair on the other side of the living room, then he took her body violently. I started crying that hard I needed my potty as I felt sick with the smell.

It was about two or three weeks later when my dad beat me black and blue because I wanted to watch dancing on the TV. I was able to do that when Dad wasn't there, as long as I was in bed when he came home. But this particular night he came home early and in a foul mood. I was crying on the stairs because Mum said she wanted me in bed early, and I wasn't allowed to watch dancing that night. When Dad came home he walked by me, asked Mum what I was crying for, and she told him. So he got hold of me and took me upstairs into my bedroom, and then he started beating me. When he finished doing what he did to me, he went downstairs and started on Mum.

**The Day I Became a Woman**
It was about a week and a half after having the electric back on I
began my first menstrual cycle. I told Mum, and she explained to
me what I should expect, and told me about becoming a grown
up. She couldn't tell me much as he was in the room listening,
but that night when I was in bed I heard Mum telling Dad, then
I heard Dad say I should go on the pill to keep me regular. Mum
told him no, not yet, to let me have my first cycle. But Dad was
getting worried, and giving reasons for me to go on the pill so
early. Mum told him I wasn't that stupid, as I was only 15 years
old, then he left and went out. After Mum and Dad finished
talking about what I should do or shouldn't do, my cycle stopped.
I had no more, apart from a little here and there.
So Dad thought it was okay for him have sex before I started
again, and he did what he always did.

After I still didn't see anything of my cycle for at least another
four weeks, I was thinking I might be with child. This really scared
me, because Dad was the only one who used to touch me.
One day when Mum was out I confronted Dad, and I told him I'd
not had my cycle for a while. He didn't worry or panic, he just
turned around and said if I was with child, I wasn't to say it was
his, and I wasn't to get him involved. But if mum found out the
child was his, he would kill us both. I would have to say someone
else got me pregnant. But after he said what he did, my flow
started again, what a relief!

## HINDSIGHT AND PERSEVERANCE
by Karen

Sometimes in life you go through something before you know
what you're going through,
Sometimes in life you gotta just keep going before you can understand what's happened to you,
Sometimes in life you go through something, and something gets
taken from you before you've had a chance to know it's being
taken away, but by the time you realise, it's already too late.

Sometimes in life you just gotta keep going.

### LONGING FOR A CONNECTION
by Karen

I give up, I give up, I don't care anymore. I can let you die wrong, let you die never having met me, having never connected, never bonded. It's all too late now.

When I was young and my voice counted for fuck all and you ran around stressed out and mad missing it all, when you weren't there to see me fall.

And you still don't get it, do you, you still don't see me, or hear me. You still don't really understand. You don't really want me, not the real me, no matter how hard I've tried,  so I'm not going to try and give myself to you anymore. We can just have meaningless, surface conversations, that to you seem so perfect and amicable, and you'll never really know me because I'm not what you really want to hear. The truth is not what you really want, you're happy believing your own lies, and sweeping it under the carpet. You deny my reality.

I'm tired, I'm tired, I'm tired of holding out for you. I've tried, I've tried, I've tried to believe that one day we would feel each other's embrace, but I'm just not what you want to hear. "Angry child," that's what you call me, what you despise. Send me away, push me away, you don't really want to know. I'm wasting my time, holding out for your hand, but you'll never understand, and you're never going to be my dad, you're never going to be my dad, you're never going to be my dad.

### RHYMING JOURNALING ONE
by Anonymous

What you don't see young'un, is you're fresh meat,

Blind to the ways of a twisted, cruel world,
They'll promise you their heart and devour your soul.

Wake up, take that darn blindfold down, 'cause you're on your
own girl, and they're eating you alive without a care in the world.

You grow up and see what you didn't before,
the penny sinks in and you'll get used no more.
That's the problem when you have no one watching,
street kids growing up broken.
They take everything they can and leave you whilst you're
choking on the pain,
when you grow up and realise the games,
and just how bad you've really been played.

I was just a child; shouldn't have been left alone to fend for
myself without a loving home.

I met an angel today, and she told me they always prey on the
weakest, that's just the way it goes,
the way of the world and the ugliness in its foes.

Now there's no going back, you can only live and learn,
to fend for yourself and save yourself the hurt.
It's easier with a hand to hold and friends who have your back,
with a man who'll treat you right, but you'll only discover that,
too late when you've already been had, looking back at the times

when those older than you, knew better than you, and your heart
was too easily up for grabs.

It's a sad world when you haven't been kept safe,
if you're blind they can betray you,
and you'll realise too late that you were used,
when you thought you were having fun, your naivety and
innocence was being abused,
it will leave you jaded,
looking back knowing you were a just a young child being
screwed over and humiliated.

You'll see, you'll understand one day though, as the tapestry
unfolds,
for all you lost they can't take your soul, and every day you carry
on fighting is one step closer to coming home.
And when you reach it you'll know,
you were born to fly, born to be true to who you are inside,
and who you are shines like the stars despite all your scars,
you're beautiful and you survived and made it through the pain
of your past.

Respect.
Never Give Up.
Peace At Last.

### RHYMING JOURNALING TWO

Please don't leave me out in the cold to grow old before I ever had a chance to enjoy being young.

Please don't leave me out here in the dark, because I'm blind and you're my only chance, because I couldn't see and I needed you to be there so I could face the traumatic reality.

Your care. That's the only chance I had, you were there and that's what matters, and now it's clearer that what's happened; won't ruin my time, not really, he screwed himself over by choosing to abuse me, my trust. I was too young to know but then again children are and that's why it's a crime, I thought I had done wrong but now I know the fault is his, not mine.

It's been difficult to see this because I was taught to take on the blame, but no child is responsible, because the adult has free will, and it's a choice to abuse a minor when you know they're not old enough to understand your twisted, cruel agenda. The desire to harm without being seen, no one but that man is responsible for himself. His choices weigh on his shoulders now, where the burden always should have been.

I am a survivor. I have been through Hell and back but I don't feel bad about who I am. I think I'm pretty all right, in fact.

I've weathered the roughest storm and stood up for myself, he didn't get away with it and I've healed my mental health.

75

What a lot to go through. Now I know it's okay to be proud of being who I am, he tried to hide me in the dark but he's the one in hiding, he's the one who is lost and trapped in the web of his own lies. It is a big trauma to have been through, but there's nothing for me to feel ashamed about; I was sexually abused as a child and I was wise enough to figure that out.

I went to the police and despite the threats I told the truth, despite the pain I managed to find help. I never gave up fighting and when he was found guilty in court I won. He looked down in shame because he knew he should be the one to feel bad about himself, and bad about what he'd done. What an awful example to set as a forty year old teacher and man. No wonder he's not welcome after committing that kind of crime. I used to think I should feel guilty but now I know I shouldn't feel bad. Now I know I deserve all the support available for being a victim of his crime. Sam didn't lie to me, she told me the truth, she stood by me and walked with me along this lonesome, cold, dark route. I've discovered I can trust myself now and love myself too, and I know I deserve to be looked after and supported by you.

### RHYMING JOURNALING THREE

Wouldn't it have been nice if you'd have been nice to me,
Wouldn't it have been a blast if you'd not been a creep,
Wouldn't it have been grand if you'd have held my hand,
Better luck hey baby next time around.

Wouldn't it be great if you'd not made that mistake,
And wouldn't it be a shame if I never dared love again,
Now I can tell I'm a normal girl that's been through Hell,
Better luck hey baby next time around.

Little girl,
Who ya gonna run to?
Who ya gonna turn to?
When the rain comes pouring in and you're out there on your
own, it ain't easy growing up in the storm when you got no one
to talk to.
Who ya gonna run to?
Who ya gonna turn to?

You're dealing with somebody who's still a little bit broken, his
grip on me was tight enough to silence the truth from being
spoken, he had me choking, and,

He did something to me, which can never be undone,
he took my heart and took my hand and told me I could trust in
him.
But he used my body, and abused my soul, and the emotional
damage on me has really taken its toll.

It tears me up on the inside; I'm sickened by what he did,
to know that I was sexually abused when I was still a kid.

I hate him for doing it. I wish he never had. I wish I'd had the
chance to fall in love with a kind young lad and share a sweet
romance.
But sometimes life's a battlefield, that'll leave you bitter with pain
too horrific to feel, and the only way to get through it, is to keep
on being real.

It doesn't matter how much I wish, I'll never change the facts.
I am a person who was sexually abused as a child, defenceless
and too young to stop the attack. The acts of violence, of rape,
of abuse, the lies I didn't understand...I was still a child needing
somebody to hold my hand.

It's the worst kind of betrayal, he stole everything I had. The only
thing he couldn't take is my will to remain true to being who I
am. He took my chances before I had the chance to know he was
taking them away.

At times I felt like I fucked it. In my rebellion he saw the chance to
blow my soul to shreds. By going against my only parent left and
dancing in the dark, he had the opportunity to steal my heart.
Now in every situation, with every person I meet, I have the job
of explaining the humiliating defeat.

Still, at times I've hidden the truth, for fear of being rejected, but
I'm not different, though going through this nightmare certainly
left me affected. A nightmare I didn't cause, at the mercy of
another's hand. A nightmare induced by someone else, when I
was too young and defenceless to understand.

At times I've felt like used goods, like an old and worn out toy,
left alone after it was broken, at the back of the cupboard
somewhere unseen and out of the way. And who wants a worn
out broken toy in this day and age? Just throw it away and buy
a new one; but I can't buy a new one of me, and I can't have my
time again, so I'm left with being this broken way, which I fear
no one will really want. And I regret more than anything trusting
the man who abused me, the man who slowly boiled me till I
was cooked alive, the one who scorched every living inch of my
innocent and trusting insides.

It wasn't safe to sleep, and it wasn't safe for me to be innocent.

What the actual fuck have I been through and how did it ever
get that bad? How was he allowed to get away with his abuse? It
really makes me mad.
To realise the lies I've been told so I would remain blind to being
treated like his piece of meat, their brains behind this body, but I
won't admit defeat.
He may have stolen my innocence and spun a web of lies, but
you'll see I've managed to figure out the truth by looking at the
confidence in my eyes.
I used to feel terrified, I thought I was to blame, I used to feel
like I had committed the worst crime in the world, but it's my
world that has swirled and twirled in and out of flashbacks, of
being abused as a young girl. Tonight it has happened, tonight I
understand, I didn't cause what he did to me, that perverted cunt
of an old man.

I am the queen of the darkness, and he's the biggest loser
here, his schemes to break my soul into a million little bits have
become perfectly clear. Nobody who's anybody will think well of
him after knowing what he did, walking around bragging about
fucking-over a little kid. I was raped as a child and the abuser
tried to blame me, but it doesn't matter what anyone says,
because I don't blame me. I was a child, and even if I wasn't,
instead an adult let's say, it's never the victims fault, if the abuser
decides to rape.

Each man is responsible for his own choices, and as a kid I was
not responsible for knowing I was being groomed, it was the
adult who was supposed to treat me right, because they already
knew the rules. He broke the rules at the expense of my entire
life, the strife, how I died inside from not being treated right.

That's how little loyalty he had towards me, and yet I stood up
and defended him, I trusted and believed in his lies, and my heart
I gave to him. But it's not in his keeping any more. My heart lies
in my own hands. They are holding and nursing it back to health
after every single wound endured. I didn't have a clue at the time
how badly I was being betrayed. I didn't even realise I was being
treated like an object or slave. How little I was valued for actually

being me, I wasn't even allowed to have my own boundaries.

I've lived without a voice, but my spirit he couldn't take, and with every hand that's held me, there's a mending of the break. I've been growing stronger, and my silence has turned into a whisper, and now it's getting louder, as my head is becoming clearer. I feel I've got it within me to shout out loud that I've been raped, and I'll feel no guilt or shame for the horrific choices someone else made. And when people ask me, no longer shall I hide, I don't give a flying cahoona if others look surprised. The truth is that it happened, some nasty fuck was shitty enough to sexually abuse me as a child, and I'm actually a fucking hero for managing to survive. What a fucking loser, to blame me for his betrayal, and he'll have all the time to realise his karma, whilst he's sitting there in jail.

# CHAPTER FOUR:  WRITINGS

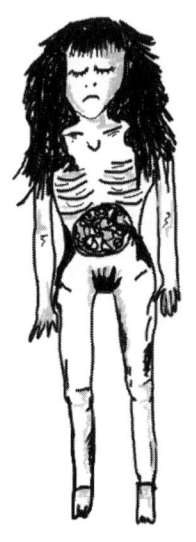

By Angela McKenzie

## I AM WHO I AM
by Usha

As I slowly watch the world go by I witness all my past wounds heal, as though they were never manifested, and the pain, deceit, selfishness, dishonesty, physical abuse never occurred. As I stand here in my present state of mind I discover self-love, the most powerful tool in existence, and with this blessing a wonderful new creation was formed. I cannot change my past, but through my mind's eye I created difference in each and every encounter displayed to me. I forgive my past, embrace my future, and enjoy my here and now with unlimited abundance, love, light, and peace. I turned my fears into ants and turned my joys into appreciation and it all emerged into—

"I am who I am."

Helping those see light through their distorted vision enables me to grow into the being I wish to be, through all my blessed trials and tribulations. I am free. I've worked hard, day and night, to cultivate my foundations as a spiritual being. I magically have the power to destroy that of which serves me no purpose with gratitude for the opportunity. Forever will I learn, thank you Universe, Spirit, God and my beautiful Angels, for your unconditional love, support and wisdom. You shine on me every single blessed day. I love you, live and let live.

### CULTIVATING THE PATTERNS
by Usha

Thousands of miles from here, a different world, maybe a
different planet,
My innocence was taken from me!  My survival kicked in, and my
walls were created.
My role as a carer, protector, my responsibilities as a daughter,
a sister, a friend, censored me from speaking the truth.
Tolerance, patience, forgiveness, isolation, self-harm, incubation,
hibernation and shame; all these negative labels have been
manifested in my mind. My spirit has been wounded but my
soul worked hard to see the lessons that I have been given. My
strengths, my determination to remain at peace with myself and
others, was challenged in extreme ways. A false sense of reality
kicked in and illusions of my existence were created in such depth
that it suppressed my growth.
But the light always shone!
There was a voice from heaven to say do not fold, you are nearly
there, victory will be yours.
Cultivating the patterns were part of the light I held onto, which
then allowed me to deal with all those labels and express my
inner child. The icing on my cake was ISAS.

## LIFE'S LESSON
by Usha

A house, a car, a great job, a string of holidays, studying! What does it all mean if my soul is at war? I'm spiritually wounded. These earthly realms are exhausting my being. The brutality of my journey here has hindered me. I can't carry on like this. I feel like I've been shot a dozen times and I'm crawling up a battlefield with a soldier above me, ready to finish me off, but instead he gloats and watches me struggle. "Just kill me," I say with what energy remains. He laughs. Instead, he pokes my eyes out so I can no longer see. He disappears. I can still hear and feel the earth beneath me, everything becomes silent. All of a sudden I take flight; I feel the warm breeze against my wounded self and scales under my hands, as if I was flying with a dragon. It puts me down on a fluffy cloud of healing, my bodily pain (the bullets) has gone and the wounds are healed. I have movement as I did at birth, but my eyes stay closed as my heart begins to heal from the detrimental experiences. I'm back home where it all began.

## DARK OR LIGHT
by Usha

Censored, while discreetly being abused, surrounded by people.
Shocked into imprisonment and frozen into a living corpse. As my
eyes well up in fear, and my teeth left imprints on my lips, my toes
curled, my stomach felt sliced by a butchers knife. I was crucified
and decapitated alive as he glared into my eyes with pleasure
and silent control, knowing I would not say a word. I became a
hopeless victim of sexual abuse. It went on for some time and I
couldn't do anything about it, because my voice had been stolen,
my body had been chained. It was infested by insects crawling all
over and I didn't have the will power to remove them, leeches
sucked the life out of me. I walked alongside the dead.
Smile and pretend it never happened. I can't bear this enclosure
any longer, it's unbearable and my whole existence will be
destroyed by the power of insecure men. It infuriates me so
much. They will never get away with this. I feel numb...

## FREE SPIRIT
by Usha

I am a Sikh girl who has the right to be happy and live a peaceful life. I've listened to everything I have ever been told to do. Never a good way to live, like a robot. Eat this! Okay. Sit down! Okay. Stand up! Okay. Go shop! Okay. Be abused! Okay. It led to self-destruction. Though I am blessed enough to step back and assess my life's patterns and change them now, it's been a turbulent ride for sure. But I now understand that my journey here is actually a huge eye opener. I am a spiritual being who through my blessed counsellors have come to the realisation that I am worth something. I am nobody's scapegoat and I should be proud of the way I have handled myself as a humble being. Life is an opportunity to live, or not. Our traumas, labels, and pressures are external. We can choose to emphasise our thoughts if we wish to. New boundaries need to be implemented and displayed. Our opportunities are abundantly ours, when our hearts are healed from the pain of others. We are survivors, warriors, supreme beings. Love, and let live.

## I AM FINALLY FREE
### by Usha

Counselling saved my life, my future, and my spirit, and is the most natural way to solving and cultivating the darkest nights of our souls. Through all of my trials and tribulations here on this earth plane, I finally felt it was my time to really start to deal with these great denials. They served a purpose for years, but no longer belonged in my mind, body or soul. I faced life and death, and my mind became a terrifying place to live in. An arctic isolation was being formed in my mind's eye, so it became a case of fight, flight or night. I needed to fly; I'd been through far too much to fold now. I can do this, I will do this, I owe it to myself to honour me, instead of these experiences that have left my soul injured. Counselling enabled me to be brave and feel safe. I have a weekly check-in and their loving support was just what my soul required. As frightening as it felt I knew I could no longer be a slave to my subconscious. My life after opening this can of worms, the magnitude of all sorts of emotions, became extremely turbulent. I kept moving and releasing until now these experiences no longer hinder me, they have allowed me to be grateful for all I have been through. Thank you universe, thank you counsellors.

## RECOGNISING
by Usha

Now that I am an adult, I've finally come to terms with the truth of being sexually abused by three of my so-called family members. For many years I convinced myself that I needed to do as I was told, as a young Asian girl that was expected. I was helping make somebody happy, men are always right. Neither of these statements are true. So although my soul knew it was an indecent act against my will, I allowed it because I was an Indian girl being told by an adult what to do. I knew better but wasn't brave enough to voice it.

So I buried it...

Decades later, I knew I had to face the demons the perAnonymoustors had created. It has by no means been easy, but it has been crucial for my journey of healing.

## CENSORED
by Usha

Terrified! I was sixteen years old. My kindness was mistaken for willingness to enter a no-zone area.

He slowly worked his ways with me. I thought he was a caring uncle! He was nothing but a paedophile, nonce, child abuser, a sick, twisted person. But nevertheless, a human being that had no good guidance. Horrified, censored and very alone, sheer survival had to kick in as nobody could know about this, because I would be the one to blame.

Protecting my baby sisters from this human being became my mission. For three months he tormented me, and I couldn't mutter a single word about it. I suffered in silence. Now, twenty years later I can finally spread my wings and remove this burden. Enough is enough!

### Father Forgive Me:
### The Truth Behind Catholic Education,
### Bigotry and Abuse
by Joe

The Roman Catholic Church accounts for 10% of schools in the United Kingdom and as such is a permanent fixture in the education of British Children. For many people this is a non-issue. After all, schools are primarily there to educate, not condition, children. That seems to be the common consensus. Based on this consensus, millions of parents leave their children as wards of this system every day, expecting them to be cared for, protected and educated to the highest of standards. Their trust is implicit but sadly, is not always honoured. I experienced that first hand. "There is something fundamentally wrong with you." That is the starting point. In accordance with the doctrine of original sin we are all born in a manner that requires us to be in a state of constant repentance for we are "fallen" in nature. It is hard to believe, but it is essential for the survival of the church that this be taught to people at as young an age as possible. It is, after all, integral to them that people live in fear, for it is only through fear that we will obey.

I remember being exposed to this from a very young age. Although my parents were in no way religious, I was sent to Catholic School because of its high acclaim, and as such was subject to their beliefs and rituals. Every day would begin with the "Our Father", a prayer requesting forgiveness for the "sins" which we supposedly committed each and every day.

For a rational, thinking adult such words should not really hold any fear. However, as a child going through their parent's divorce, the damage caused by hearing you are fundamentally flawed each and every day is immense. It can be hard enough to avoid self-blame during family crises, but to have that sense of self-doubt reinforced in you each and every day makes it near-on impossible.

Children are full of insecurities; it is a natural part of childhood development. But the truth is that being part of a system that reinforces these insecurities can make them difficult to let go of as you get older. After all, such insecurities can be validated all too easily in a world in which you are born into the influence of the Devil.

As a young man I began to challenge those in authority more often. My naturally analytical mind turned me away from religion and towards philosophy. At the age of ten I had already developed my own concept of what God would be if he were a reality. Humanity was a chess-game, controlled by its omnipotent game master, indifferent to the souls and lives of their pieces unless they could stand to gain something.

I left primary school with this mindset. Too young to yet discard the notion of a higher power, but too old (before my time) to buy into the concept of an all loving father figure high above in the clouds. What I didn't realise then was that the minor ceremonial nature of my prior school would be nothing compared to the insidious underlying shame that would become part of my everyday life.

From the beginning of my teenage years, I knew that I was different to the other kids. It wasn't just that I was more introverted, although that was undoubtedly difficult in what was very much a "macho" environment. It was something more fundamental. After years of struggling I realised, and accepted, that I was gay and in so doing unknowingly set myself up for what was one of the worst years of my life.

To say homosexuality was a taboo subject at our school would be an understatement of the highest order. It was deliberately and authoritatively avoided. The personal prejudices of certain members of staff, combined with their fear of legal repercussions, meant that they knew that they had to keep their silence on the topic, but it seeped through into school life regardless.

Our school was forced by government mandate to issue "some form" of sexual education, but needless to say, it didn't really apply for a young gay man. It's not that I was expecting a "How-To Guide" of gay life. However, it would have been nice if the one mention of being gay wasn't the "fact" that gay men were considerably more likely to catch sexually transmitted diseases due to their natural proclivity for promiscuity.

Homophobic abuse by other children was considered par for the course and certainly not something that would be classified as "true bullying". It was merely boys being boys and certainly not worth taking any further. Regularly during lessons comments would be made about me that teachers would simply choose not to hear. Not that I particularly wanted them to, as things were difficult enough without being considered a charity case by people who did not care either way.

Indeed homophobic "humour" wasn't considered a step too far even for members of staff. Like most people of my age I developed feelings for a pupil within my year, a fact which certain people found it entertaining to report to the entire year. I would find out later this individual's apparent deep resentment for me stemmed from the fact that a particular teacher felt it an entertaining anecdote to make reference to during lessons. Something which was again simply put down to "boys being boys," or I suppose in this case, "men being men".

It is important to say that not all members of staff were guilty of this, or even a majority. Indeed two of my teachers were integral in helping shape me into the man I am today. My Drama teacher (somewhat of a cliché, I suppose) had a soft spot for me and my flair for the dramatic. Indeed it was through my often avant garde (and perhaps somewhat insane) creative projects that I was able to express the part of me that so many others wished me to keep quiet.

My English teacher, too, convinced me from a young age that I had a talent for writing and that I should pursue it. More than that, though, she taught me that I mattered, that my opinion had value and I should always express it, no matter how much it grated on the authorities above me. I remember on the day I left high school she saw how upset I was (not because of leaving, but for other reasons) and even though she didn't know, she seemed to understand when she said, "It will get better when you leave here, you know?"

But in spite of these few inspirations, the school atmosphere was very difficult on a daily basis. Every day I had to walk down four flights of stairs and read the large sign that greeted all students entering the R.E. Department—

"Homosexuality....Alternative Lifestyle or
Abomination Before God?"

You would think that such a pejorative statement—actually, scratch that—such a blatant insult, would have been considered blatant discrimination. However, each and every year the school would fly through its OFSTED inspection with its inevitable "Outstanding" grade.

Indeed, our school's natural inclination for denial and cover-ups contributed greatly to their repeated successes in national inspections. Every year, regular as clockwork, our "less able" students were moved to the other side of the school for their lessons and the inspectors were paraded around our Top-Set classes to make their observations. As with my "lifestyle," (as they so beautifully described it), the school ensured its "undesirables" were kept far away from prying eyes.

However, such rudimentary exercises to appease inspectors couldn't compare to some of the other issues that this devoutly Christian institution felt were best kept away from the public. The same teacher who found my own life so apparently entertaining would be the same individual who was asked to "disappear" from the school after a nightclub liaison with a fifteen year old pupil. All meetings that day were held behind closed doors and the sight of the girl sobbing certainly didn't seem to suggest to them that he had done anything wrong. Publicly, he merely requested a release from his contract, for "personal reasons."

It would be this mindset that would result in me suffering the worst of my experiences. During my final year of high school, I would be repeatedly and routinely sexually abused by a fellow pupil. A kingpin of the "macho" stylings prevalent throughout the year, he merely treated me as a toy. His actions, of which he would regularly publicly brag, were intended to prove he could have anyone he wanted, boy or girl. There was never any question of his sexuality, he merely had a point to prove about the power he held, and prove it he did.

He would regularly grope me and wrench my hand onto his own body to "return the favour." Eventually, bored of this, he would force his hand beneath my waistband and again force me to do the same to him, all the while telling me how much I "loved it." In spite of the fact that this abuse took place during lessons and in front of students, it was somehow never "discovered" by members of staff. After all, it wouldn't have done their reputation much good to have their Rugby Captain accused of molesting another boy, as such things could never happen on such holier than thou ground.

So I was dragged through my final year. Aside from all this, I was being regularly called in front of the Head of Year for being a "bully," an accusation made by the same girl who took it upon herself to "out" me to the entire school the year prior. Her actions were, of course, justifiable in the eyes of God... after all, why not point out the "abomination?" It was my retaliation that was a step too far in their eyes.

In those final months I began to realise how little I meant to that establishment as a person. My ten year old ethos had been vindicated; I was a piece in a game whose only value was my instrumentality in the school's success. As I was once told by the headmistress after failing to get an A Grade in German (in spite of achieving straight A's in all other subjects) it was about "money" and nothing else. I remember having a begrudging level of respect for her for finally having the guts to admit it out loud. Verbally abused for failing to make grades and regularly humiliated in front of my peers, I was finally forced to endure the last charade. The leaving "Ball." As I sat there, humiliated and broken down by a year of hell, I had to watch while that same rugby Captain who repeatedly abused me, climbed the podium to accept award after award, including a "Gag Award" for "Campest Rugby Player." Everyone in that room knew what that was for; it was a reference to the "relationship" he had had with me, and he was getting an award for it.

So there it was. The bigotry and hypocrisy of the Catholic Church, laid bare in one of their highest ranked national institutions. The regularly "Outstanding" Catholic High School, that gave an award to a sexual abuser while informing his victim that his "lifestyle" may confuse other children.

Society is changing now, and I recognise that, but I am also no fool. The Catholic Church never has, and never will, change. It will always be a haven for the depraved practices and outrageous bigotries of its occupants, constantly surviving through its parasitic dependence on fear and obedience.

It is this institution that controls 10% of the education of British Children. This cult of deception, bigotry, fear and denial, is being allowed to maintain its death grip on the youngest members of our society and there's no one to speak out.

After all, when you're already "fallen"...what's the point?

## MY STORY
By Angela

I don't remember much. I have some flashes, some moments engrained on my brain that I think about over and over again, but so much of that time has been erased or buried in my subconscious. Sexual abuse and violence. But I survived. My sexual abuse was always like a game, and I was always praised for the things I did, so I liked it and this is my shame. I was so desperate for love and affection and praise that I wanted to 'perform well' in those sex games.

Let's meet the characters in the story. First, my mum. She is damaged and has never recovered. The things that she has experienced has poisoned her soul so much that she *is* her damage. In every cruel word and deed she is her own living, breathing monster, throwing her pain and self-hate around with relish and a desperate need to hurt others, for her own catharsis. I get this now, and I think I forgive her. In so many ways she is magnificent. Driven by such deep, dark feelings she is a woman who can do, and does, extraordinary things. That she could never get well is a tragedy and a waste of a great woman.

My dad. He is damaged, but his monster lives inside him like a separate personality; A personality he appears to have no awareness of and cannot, or will not, take responsibility for. He is two people. One is a lost, insecure and bullied little boy and the other is full of rage and hate, a savage and violent ogre. Never the twain's have met. So, for as long as I can remember my Dad

105

has been a violent man, but with no rhyme or reason. One of my earliest memories is of my brother bent over the sofa while beaten with a cane by my dad, as my mum egged him on like it was masturbation for her.

He is also desperately lonely. A man who wants to be loved and respected, but his other personality destroys all possibility of that. So he lives a sad, lonely, bitter life that he created.
My brothers: Both victims. Stewart was the first born, so unlucky. He was dealt the full force of my parent's sickness and cruelty for eight years before I was even born and they poisoned him by making him the chalice for their self-loathing. They told him, and themselves, that he was 'born evil' and sought to beat it out of him. He grew, unsurprisingly, into a disturbed and delinquent young man, and to this day he too believes he was 'born evil,' and plays the part to perfection as an alcoholic, wife beater, and violent child abuser. He will never be well, and I think it will be a relief when he finally manages to drink himself to death. Although, in his lucid moments he reveals his deep longing for my parents love and approval, and I can only imagine how much his heart was repeatedly broken and torn. He will never be fixed.
Cameron, the second born and the 'golden boy.' Adored, exulted, abuser and abused. His experiences and his feelings about them are locked away inside him, although I do know he went to the doctors once to beg for help. He found a way out, tried to be a normal boy, tries to be a normal man. He had some freaky nervous ticks when he was young, as a response to the trauma, so I know it was huge. So huge that he has re-written his entire life story to be able to cope. I know he feels guilt. He told me once that he wished he had been the first born. Maybe he could have saved us.

He has a wife and kids and money now. He is a good father and has built the opposite of what he comes from. But I am the sacrificial lamb in his survival plan. I hold the truth about his life in my memory, so he has removed from his life, written me out so he doesn't have to look at me and remember. It's the only way he can survive. He has daughters though, and I wonder if he ever thinks of me.

Then came me. So innocent, but that didn't last. I remember the filthy, stinking hovel we had to call a home. I remember the chaos and almost constant rage in the house. I remember feeling detached, or feeling nothing. I remember a feeling of constant misery, or simply an absence of happiness. I was not sugar and spice and all things nice. I remember being not very normal at all. But here I am.

There have been many times when I thought I wouldn't make it, and times when I have crossed my heart and hoped to die. Times when I thought remembering would kill me, and times when I have lived wildly just to see if I could have an unfortunate accident.

The only thing that has stopped me from 'leaving' is my little sister. It would have hurt her too much, and although her life has not been perfect, I want to protect and preserve the one piece of purity that has managed to grow in the stinking bile that is my family.

My parents were sick when they met; this is what drew them together and has kept them together all these years. They cannot see beyond their sickness. Their house, our house, was and is a perfect reflection of their inner workings and their children: vessels to vomit their putrid filth into.

The things I remember...
Firstly, the filth. Our house was a disgusting, filthy pit. No cleaning was ever done, but I remember my mum often running around the house screaming hysterically about the mess, how it was all our fault, and how she COULDN'T COPE!

We always had cats and dogs. We lived in a small three bedroom council house. Two parents, three kids, two cats and two Alsatians. Often, it felt as if the dogs took up the whole space, with their filthy breath and stinking drool. I hated them. Mostly, I hated the dog piss and shit on the kitchen floor every morning for years and years and years. They weren't cared for properly either, but were locked in the kitchen, forced to stay under the kitchen table and rot. Consequently, they didn't have the chance to do their business outside. Every morning, the kitchen floor would be covered in the yellow, acid-smelling piss of two dogs, and their shit in a myriad of forms. Once, I came down in the morning and a long white worm was flipping about in the dog's diarrhoea, an internal parasite dying on my kitchen floor. I stopped eating at home.

I remember we had some crazy red patterned carpet, but you wouldn't be able to tell, as it was constantly coated in a thick layer of tan and black Alsatian hair. I remember Cameron brought a girlfriend home once. I could see the look of shock and disgust on her face as we all pretended to be a nice normal family.

## SHATTERED SOUL
by Chloe

One touch was all it took to shatter my soul into a million pieces. A broken mirror has a distorted reflection. It sounded like laughter as those pieces fell to the ground, and he smiled. Did you know that shame literally burns? Like being in the seventh circle of hell, engulfed by flames. I kicked off every blanket and still it scorched. It seared and blistered.

He was poison in my veins. Killing me slowly from the inside out. Because when nothing remains inside, I destroy myself from the outside, using the shards of my broken soul to draw pictures of my shattered life, all in red on a flesh covered canvas. And every knife was a star, glinting in the dark, beckoning me closer with the promises of anything, anything better than this. I knew they were lying and still I couldn't stop. There was a chance to breathe five minutes before the guilt hit me like a tidal wave.

I was only ever his little string puppet. He controlled every aspect of my life, all of my mind. A puppet, one of many, with tangled strings and broken limbs. Watching our masters as they laugh, waiting in the shadows that protect them from retribution. A sick joke I can never understand. I sewed my lips shut with black thread, because why scream when no one will listen? In the labyrinth of his twisted psyche, inescapable, I saw myself as he saw me; an object, washed away down the plughole while he kissed my mother, with me on his lips. And the tears that should have fallen sizzled to insignificance on the heat of my shame.

The mirror is not fixed, the shards still cut me, and still he laughs.

I guess it's funnier from where he stands, free to see me locked in the prison cell of my own mind, chained to my own relentless memory.

# CHAPTER FIVE: GROUP COLLABORATIONS

By Angela McKenzie

### CULTIVATION

Alive and kicking—and here we stand.
Battered and bruised, downtrodden and used.
Controlled in an environment that should be free,
Doubted and not heard... No one listens to me.
Exploited and used, controlled and abused.
Fear without tears, not heard through the years,
Guilty for being there, guilty that I did not share.
Hurting my heart, full of sorrow and pain,
I ask myself now, am I going insane?
Innocence so sweet, but now incomplete,
Judged by others, unfairly condemned, this happened to me!
It didn't to them!

Kicked and punched till black and blue,
I hid it well. Nobody knew.
Lonely is the feeling I have left inside,
Misery and sadness you left behind.
Night time is the hardest of all to bear,
It leaves you scared and full of fear.
Objects you put in my way,
Making it hard for me to survive the day.

Like a predator you had me trapped,
Stuck in a corner, there was no way out.
Quiet as a mouse you had to be,

Hidden from sight, no one could see.
Remembering the things that he has done,
All for his enjoyment and his fun.
Suffering in silence, letting no one know,
Suffering in silence, just putting on a show.
Tormented and teased, they made my life hell,
Under your power, under your thumb,
You hurt me too, not only mum.

Victory was mine as I got away,
I finally got a chance to have my say!
The warrior I have become,
Standing brave and feeling strong.
X-ray: you can see straight through them,
If they have bad bones you should avoid them.
Years of abuse I have endured,
Now I've put a stop to it, there is no more.
Zest for life that I have found,
Blessed by light my soul abounds.

## Anger

When anger enters into my mind,
Should I be angry or should I be kind?
But I was blind, the trusting kind,
And now it's a blind innocence of time.

His violence, my silence,
Bites the skin until it's sore.
Can smoke, can drink, I've done it all,
All mixed up—I told you so,
My eyes closed, he broke my soul.
Get a hammer, knock it down,
Screaming loud, without a sound.

I'm tired of suppressing rage,
Of feeling locked within a cage.
A sadistic attack done through abuse,
Fighting back, what's the use?

I want to destroy,
Something beautiful and good,
Take back what he took.
I want to tear this child down,
I want to burn him to the ground,
I want what's lost, to be found.

I'm speaking out my long suppressed sound
My valid rage no longer silenced.
Unrestricted freedom from his violence.
Can you see my strength of heart?
To stand here naked, torn apart.

## LOVE

Love is positive, uplifting,
Love is soothing, makes your body tingle.
Love is safe,
Love is trustworthy,
In love you can let go.
Love is magical,
Makes life worth living,
Love is comforting, caring and genuine,
Love is sharing,
Has others best interests at heart.

Makes you feel happy,
Makes me cry and touches my heart,
It is elevating,
Love is grounding,
Makes you do crazy things.
Love is safe,
It's a choice not to hurt others,
A choice to sooth another,
Love overrides other desires and impulses,
Love is pure and unconditional.
Love with conditions is manipulation,
If you don't do what I want,
I will withdraw my attention,
Conditional love excludes, separates, controls,
Doesn't appreciate differences—judges,
Looks down upon.
That's not love, that's control.

Love is necessary,
Without love life is like a
Desert dying of thirst.
A plant scrunched up without any water,
There is no nourishment without love.
Love is a light,
Love just feels right.
Sometimes love tells you things,
You don't want to hear.

Love is someone who's got your back.
Love grows, changes, deepens,
Becomes more insightful and powerful.
Love is the opposite of control.
If you love someone, let them go,
Love is trusting they will come back.
Love does not force,
Or make you do stuff against your will.
Love is meeting halfway,
Love is courage, great courage.
Love is like food,
Find the right one and you just can't stop eating.
Love is a tonic,
Love is a donut, hot and sweet.
Love is water, clear and cleansing,
Love is holistic,
Live is hot chocolate.
I feel happy to be loved.
Love travels,
Love stays after a person goes,
Stays alive, is everlasting.

### THE JOURNEY TO ACCEPTANCE

She was bashful, beautiful, bright, and brilliant.
Standing on the top of a mountain,
Staring up at the stars.
Inside she shone red, torn with rage.
Her resourceful nature kept her resilient.

Standing at the edge, letting the kite fly free,
At last she can alleviate her torment.
The violent wind carries her trauma.
A new life she can create by
Leaving behind her hate.
Acceptance...

Comfortable in her mind,
Hopeful in her soul.
Her angry tears falling in compassion,
She rips off her cloak of anxiety,
Worries slip away.
Her voice, once little, grows and grows,
Reclaiming its power.
At one with the roaring of the wind.

Vengeance gained through inner kindness,
Kindles a fire in her heart.
Melting the ice block,
Allowing love and laughter in.

Her story was told to the waiting wind,

Like a shoulder that cared,
Steadying and stabilising her weary mind.

As she descends, her inner-self cleanses,
She's happy and healthy.
Though she appears the same,
Her metamorphosis is now complete.
Like a butterfly she floats with the wind.

Her journey complete,
She emerged from her chrysalis.
From a place of self destruction,
She is regaining control,
Reclaiming her power,
Escaping her prison.

Winning.

The Pursuit of Freedom
by Anonymous

With Special Thanks To:

Nottingham Clinical Commisioning Group
Unsung Heroes
People's Health Trust
Nottingham Equal